'I didn't realize it was infectious.'

'THERE'S A LOT OF IT ABOUT'

Dickinson at the doctor's

Foreword by Alan Coren

COLUMBUS BOOKS
LONDON

'My legs have gone numb.'

First published in Great Britain in 1985 by
Columbus Books
Devonshire House, 29 Elmfield Road, Bromley, Kent BR1 1LT

Printed and bound by Clark Constable,
Edinburgh, London, Melbourne

ISBN 0 86287 253 7

Introduction

When, a few years and innumerable aches and pains ago, *Punch* decided to set up a monthly subsidiary entitled *Digest For Doctors* on the irreproachable Hippocratic principle that there might well be a bob or two in it, there could have been no other choice for resident cartoonist than Geoffrey Dickinson.

An editor must always see eye to eye with his artists, and never in the whole history of recorded humour has this inter-retinal sympathy been stronger than it is between Dickinson and me. That is because it is entirely literal: hardly has Dickinson hobbled through my morning door than we are gazing deeply into one another's eyes. Not for any reason that either of us need be ashamed of, but simply in order to find out what kind of shape we're in . . . are they yellow this morning, red-rimmed, conjunctivally jellied, veined like a Tube map, or merely vanished into the puckered folds of fatigue?

Dickinson and I do this because we are hypochondriacs. Over the long years of our associ-ation, we have had everything anyone has ever died of, and we have frequently had it more than once. I myself, for example, have had bubonic plague on at least three occasions, while Dickin-son has been down with typhoid four times, and smallpox, as I recall, twice. Sometimes I diag-nosed his, sometimes he diagnosed mine, but in every case we spotted it early, and it soon went away.

This major work is thus the ideal guide to medical matters: Dickinson has actually sat in 53 per cent of the nation's waiting-rooms (he and I always take the precaution, despite our mutual respect, of a second opinion), and there is nothing he does not know about doctors.

There is, of course, even less they don't know about him.

3

The waiting-room

'Of course, in the old days they only painted
your affected parts purple.'

'Been here long?'

'It's the General Medical Council –
I should let them go in first.'

5

'I'm afraid we can't correct spelling mistakes on the National Health.'

'Has anyone got a dock leaf?'

6

'I think it's rather late for standing on the seat in your case, Mr Histon.'

'I hope he's really ill and not just touting for business.'

'No, it only hurts when I have to explain how I came to fall off the wardrobe.'

8

9

'Why don't they get a digital clock?
Then we could see the date change as well.'

'Very last patient, please.'

10

In the surgery

'He's got laryngitis.'

'Well, it makes a change
from taking pans off kids' heads.'

11

'It's difficult to be 100% sure –
but at a guess I would think it's
agoraphobia.'

'If you want a second opinion, come back tomorrow.
I might have changed my mind by then.'

'Come in,
Mrs Johnson.
What is it
this week –
more of the hot
flushes?'

13

'I know there's nothing wrong with me. I keep telling you –
I-AM-THE-HEALTH-VISITOR.'

14

'Another New Year's resolution
up the spout, I'm afraid,
Miss O'Flanagan.'

'You've got that Monday morning feeling,
I've got that Monday morning feeling – sorry!
come back on Wednesday.'

15

'*Another of your cries for help, Mr Johnson?*'

16

'You don't often see tennis elbow nowadays –
it's usually dislocation of the jaw.'

'Only two bottles a day –
I don't know how
you do it, Mr Riley!'

'Morning, doctor – my wife thinks
I'm suffering from stress . . .
God, is that the time? –
let me have your views in triplicate –
can I use the phone? –
my secretary will do the medical . . .
must rush – let's
have lunch some time . . .'

18

'You need a break – why not have a week in the country and ruin a few hunts?'

'Don't tell me – kaolin and morph was useless so you tried a little sign language in a chemist's shop outside Boulogne?'

19

20

On the touchline

'I can't take him off until he tells me his BUPA number.'

'The last time I used this stuff on a strain,
the horse won the Cheltenham Gold Cup
half an hour later.'

'I told you to pace yourself, doc.'

'Tell me the worst, doc –
will I have to play in the second half?'

'Don't worry –
they can do wonders
for hangovers nowadays.'

23

At the barbers

'What a coincidence – I used to go out
with a prop forward from Barts.'

'A student will be dealing with you this morning.'

'Blood group?'

'Anything for the weekend?'

'We don't do transplants, you know, doc . . .'

26

Student doctors

'Well, your diagnosis is absolutely correct –
I was hoping you'd suggest a cure.'

'She left me for one of my own students –
and he suddenly came top in gynaecology.'

28

'Nigel, wouldn't it be quicker if your father carved as usual?
It's half past four.'

29

'He's either dead or my stethoscope
is full of fluff again.'

'This student thinks your accident on a building site
is probably hereditary, Mr O'Shaunessy.'

'One hundred and eighty!'

Bogus doctor

*'I won't tell the unions that you're a private patient
if you won't tell them that I'm a bogus doctor.'*

*'Yes, for a bogus doctor he
certainly had a very good grasp of anatomy.'*

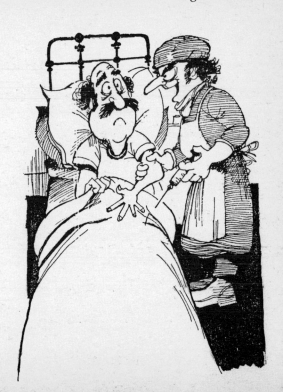

'Of course I'm qualified – I got my City
and Guilds in plastering at
Brixton College of Building.'

'Of course I know
he's bogus,
but as I'm a malingerer . . .'

'At a glance – I'd say 100th-of-a-second at f8.
That dark bit is probably camera shake.'

'He's bogus, I tell you! – Will nobody believe me? He's bogus!'

34

On holiday

*'We were going on holiday to a Greek island, but my dad
didn't like the look of the hospital in the brochure.'*

'Hey! It must be my lucky day – sitting next to a doctor all the way to Bermuda.'

'I expect all this waiting around for hours with no information is all new to you, doctor?'

'Three enlarged livers, two umbilical hernias –
one possible prostate . . . '

'You're deliberately setting the children against my mother – vaccinating them every time we go to stay there.'

38

'Lobster pick – pincers – mayonnaise . . .'

'*I forgot to turn off Mrs Johnson's drip before we came away.*'

'If you're here, and Nigel and Arthur are in France, who's running the practice?'

'*Quick, let me out – I'm a doctor.*'

'Somebody around here is wearing
a blasted pacemaker.'

'I took out a piece of his small intestine that long.'

'I know you've forgotten your trunks,
but is that the best you can do?'

Doctor's wedding

'As the bride seems rather late – could you have a look at this swelling on my knee?'

'I hear she is honeymooning with a doctor from his deputizing service.'

'We would like to thank Casualty for icing the cake.'

'That's poor Fiona – she even saw him
privately but he still didn't marry her.'

46

School doctor

'Could you just give him a placebo, preferably with a very large needle – and at Assembly?'

'If I were you, I'd forget A-level Classics and change to Home Economics – you've got about eight months.'

'I'd like to see you privately –
I'm the maths master
from the boys' school.'

48

'Mind you – I don't see many prostate cases in the 11-16-year-olds.'

'I can't take it off, it's my life support system.'

'Hey – this looks great! How long does impetigo last?'

'You must try to cut down on your smoking and drinking, particularly during lessons.'

'I'd like a quick course of anabolic steroids – I'm having a fight with Ginger Kelly on Tuesday.'

'I give up – what's it say?'

At the wheel

'No specific symptoms – just a high temperature and a general lack of energy.'

'It's impossible to explain what's wrong in layman's language.'

53

'Is this under warranty or are you
going private?'

'You'd better make that 5 gallons of boiling water – and
clear a space on the counter.'

54

Showbiz doctors

'They're singing a song about my hysterectomy.'

'. . . a GP from Reigate who will answer questions on the illnesses of Mrs Edna Smythe, from 1949 to the present day . . .'

'If I'm the token patient on the programme and you're the token doctor, who's he?'

'As your delivery will be on Channel 4, could you try
to time your contractions to the commercial breaks?'

'Of course I'd still like to practise – but what
with radio, TV and book signings . . .'

'Not only is that clown my consultant – those are my gallstones he's juggling with.'

59

Dr Greenfinger

'I think I've found the swine!'

'Terribly exciting – the big one's only been fed on a placebo.'

'There's a fortune to be made for the man who comes up with a branch transplant operation.'

'I've tried everything – dried blood, horse manure, but
it was hopeless – died this morning.'

62

At the dentist

'Now, if you look into the doctor's mouth, you'll see what happens if you don't clean your teeth properly.'

'I'd no idea you were Australian, let alone a woman – I've just come to talk about a friend's dental problems.'

63

'I wanted to be a doctor but they said I was
temperamentally unfitted – ME! –
temperamental, ME!'

'The dentist's away –
I'm his deputizing service and plumber.'

'No, it's not whisky – the children have bought you two pints of blood.'

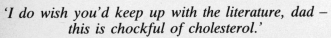

'I do wish you'd keep up with the literature, dad – this is chockful of cholesterol.'

'My own senior partner won't be coming – he says he never makes house calls over Christmas.'

The morning after

'Don't worry, don't worry – they're only arguing about who goes to get the Alka-Seltzer.'

'You haven't seen Mrs Smythe's specimen
anywhere, have you?'

'Let me guess, sir – you're a brain surgeon on his
way home from an emergency operation
at the golf club?'

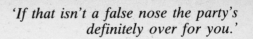

'If that isn't a false nose the party's definitely over for you.'

'Being breathalyzed ten times in three days is bound to make your chest rough.'

'You're sure this will work? –
Now, what seems to be the trouble?'

Sharp practice

'You're lucky – he's waived his fee
to make a loss in his first tax year.'

'After flying us 4000 miles in his private jet, I think the Emir was hoping for something better than two aspirins and a hot drink.'

'This won't take long – my visitor's visa expires in half an hour.'

'My next clinic is in April – or there's one
next week in the Cayman Islands if you prefer.'

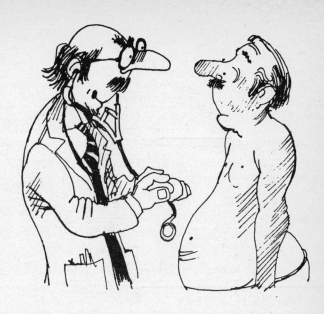

'Your problems stem from your being too rich,
but I think I can help.'

'There's nothing wrong with me – it's just a dodge so my husband can claim the holiday on expenses.'

'You'd think that with a practice this size
somebody could cure the coffee machine.'

Affairs of the heart

'George, you're not still having an
affair with your theatre sister, are you?'

'We can't go on meeting like this – my prostate
cleared up three years ago.'

'Doctor couldn't make it –
I'm his deputizing service.'

'My wife is asking for a divorce – she found
a copy of your ECG in my wallet.'

'This is my mother, my surrogate mother, my AID father, my father and my step-father.'

'Doctor Freud says there's a lot of it about.'

Acknowledgements

Punch Digest for Doctors
Primary Health Care
British Journal of Hospital Medicine
Financial Times